THE FLOATING GARDEN

The FLOATING GARDEN

D. G. JONES

COACH HOUSE

© D.G. Jones, 1995

Published with the assistance of the Canada Council, the Ontario Arts Council,
the Department of Canadian Heritage and the Ontario Publishing Centre.

First Edition
Printed in Canada
1 3 5 7 9 8 6 4 2

Canadian Cataloguing in Publication Data

Jones, D. G. (Douglas Gordon), 1929–
The Floating Garden

Poems.
ISBN 0–88910–473–5

I. Title.

PS8519.033F53 1995   C811'.54   C95–930763-X
PR9199.3.J65F53 1995

CHRISTMAS/
GOING ON

i)

Teenage girls throw their passionate
bodies on the rails, old couples
share a blanket and their bones

terminal forms of
transport, housing, or whatever
ministry of desire

Surely there is a god of laughter weighs
the pursuit of excellence
or orgasm

and the fallen crab, bright
in a Christmas rain
                          pitiful nothing
pitiless thing
                  these are small apples
the old who touch, the young
who throw their bodies
under trains

garbage in the light
of a fizzled star

And now the rain
turns to fat flakes, inters
weeds, rails, the delicate

dead grasses—ah, we say
a white Christmas

Between pity and laughter (and
the approximate seasons) there must be
another word

ii)

What was he talking about

Today is all bluster
bits of blue and then the world
disappears

the snow lifted into the sky
taking parts of houses, old pines
waving farewell

the ascension

hardly distinguishable from
the Dies Irae

and windchimes like a harmonious chaos

To touch and
to throw it away

iii)

suddenly clear
and with the stars we get television's
highlights of Christmas past

and the deportees
abiding in the fields between
Jerusalem and Beirut

no man's land and the shepherds
of the Intifada

'these boots were made for walking
and they'll walk all over you'

What was her name, the girl
who sang that?

the young Elvis

and The Choir of Life, live

silent night

the winking tail-lights of a car
index of trees
on the far side of the lake—faith

that the lake exists

of the elderly poet under his lamp
next door, hope
he put in a tree, planted, charity
towards words

        We abide
in fragments

iv)

it's touch and go

for the girls
under trains, for the rains
turned to snow

for the chickadees
that remain through the winter

the young and the old
in their blankets on the cold
hillside

it's touch and go

for the tree with its lights
and tinsel, the absent friends
no amends

to be made to the garden

the jokes, the songs
the billabongs—agh!

it's archaic
man, it's sick, slow fiddles
in the best hotels

make it, man
in the sunset streets, that's
touch and go

v)

holy night—so
it's an incantation

the girls, amid so many desires
satisfied
open a space

those huddled in blankets
simplify

helicopters on the hillside
vacant yards

between the infinite and the minimal, there is
latitude

for old words, mercy mild
hullabaloo, these boots
were made for walking and some day
they'll walk all over you

timor mortis conterbat me

a little jazz for those who pay
the barman for his company

vi)

some go to sing carols
hymns (their voices, says M
clearer at 20 below

some go to the beach
go to town, some
hear rasta talk, hear rap, hear boy
go rat-a-tat-tat for sky man
say leave your daddy, leave your mom
follow the man, no brown nosin
no bad dope, no preach placin his hope
in your pocket, heaven in your ah, ah
dress, your skin
lotion, lips and hip motion, your pa-
pillary glands, baby, we
ain't sellin you no
big hotel, no swell
condo, beach house, vehicle with air
man, this is colour, each his own, ah yes
fresh as a baby's bum
skin tone, does not rub off, lasts
forever, you can
walk on water
     —walking home, some
say still
sounds like snakeoil, some
zap the channel

some question the walls, call it a wrap

some in their blankets say Mohammet
can't even get to the mountain

some say nothing, carolling
silence (dumbsong

vii)

it's touch and go

the problem is syntax, words
old and new like the stars
registering (what
is your address, mam, sir, how
do you intend to pay) a
red shift

ave atque vale

and the choir begins to sound like
long wave radio or a requiem in
outer space or
under the sea—some
ghost of Boulez or

the void

(it may be the mother of beauty and
a few other things, say
Cleopatra and her infinite variety, but
one must approach it
gingerly; it authors
everything—the frozen mole
on the path this morning

brief finished works, abandoned
rail lines, terminals
beginning now to touch us like
old postcards—and this, this
you undertake to praise

viii)

this day (by
arbitrary calculation) is
Christmas

the choirs silent

the lake, at midday and for hours
a howling cauldron, is
silent

this day
adds a few flakes, freshening
the dead, the

living, a night
in a bad year, a night
bringing cheer or cheerful oblivion
to many

I hear a snicker
somewhere, somewhere
we

don't intend
to die

whoever we are, I'm relieved
the late farce
allows me to go to bed

without news

ix)

the happy face of the computer

desire

like the cold clarity of the New Year

the gods laughing

it is the cup that like a miracle
is bottomless
and overflows, and goes
on and on

lava, larvae, love and loneliness
and lamb chops,
broccoli and Barishnykov

a cornucopia that snows
us under, kids
starved or anorexic or

suicidal, still

what else to turn us toward the sun

on a bright day
in the year of the rooster
                              harmony
wholeness and radiance
says the purblind author

hah, it's touch
and go

desire and the multinationals, faxing
Tokyo

x)

the dinosaurs died
not exactly a capitalist error
or patriarchal hubris

the snow
the freezing rain, meteorites
may be fatal

there are, Mr. President
so-called
ecological factors

'acts of god' in the parlance
of the insurers
                and the frogs
and the cod, are they gone
with the passenger pigeon

at least the chickadees are faithful
all year round
even the furry squirrels

one feeds them if one can

still, still, how are the teeming young
to find home in the jostling
global installation, our towers and lines
communication lines and battle lines and bread lines
and lines of credit, where we trade
your heavenly mansion for
my heavenly mansion at
market prices

it has nothing to do with the decision of sparrows
or young girls
or god
        what we want
is an accurate forecast

xi)

so my back wheels are in some
lady's creek, the front end
spinning snow

who's going to pay for this
she asks, as I ask
to borrow a shovel—can't you read

there's a small notice
on the window of a truck blocking
the main drive

I'm just trying to get
to the hardware store—Christ
you discover

the weakness of front-wheel drive

the store closed

and the strength of youth
two teenagers push
without asking who's going to pay for the grass

lady, thanks for the shovel

the big guy had to put his duffel bag
in the car, first—what
I wonder, does he pack there

no problem

it's only twelve below, the small guy's happy
me too, wheeling the car
back on the plowed road

xii)

girls
I think you missed it

xiii)

life is the raw material
of art

many are called but few
are chosen

I would not embarrass the divine
market economy

the girls
were not pretty

not, perhaps, an addition
to the image bank

and yet

xiv)

nebo plachet/ bezuderzhno ... : 'I will lie down/ light/ in
lazy attire/ on the soft bed of real dung/ and the train's
wheels will embrace my neck/ while I quietly kiss the
knees of the rails.'—Mayakovsky (cited in Svetlana Boym,
Death in Quotation Marks, 129-130)

the defense admits
revenge, resentment, romantic
narrative and other
forms of false faith, the comrade's
sworn loyalty

childish honour

as well as poverty, puberty, pimples
maybe motivated their
final act

in part

alone, together, powerless, together
out of touch, in touch

they lay down on the track, neither bound
nor waiting for the hero of the silent
films—or if they were
they mistook the literacy of their boyfriends

guardians

we submit
the higher court should recognize their claim
to stardom, put their names
in lights

xv)

it's thirty below and even your mink
can't protect your face

the dead create a draught

last month they opened the Paris Metro
to the homeless
the underground has its attractions

the high heavens are cold
like the image, man

if you're rich you can opt for cryogenic
preservation

how many million years would it take
to get through the ice-age

still, the day was brilliant

a squirrel died, the dog depositing the corpse
on the white lawn

others raided the feeder

'we are words
that have lost their meaning' (Norris, K.

since they never had any
outside their relation to others, what
does this mean

like the Word, we must be absolute
and empty or
shifty, promiscuous, wholly
intertextual

        happily
my daughter called

xvi)

metaphysics is nothing, the ultimate
form of capital

we shall all strike it rich, meanwhile
if briefly, we live

an interference, manifesting
empty light

and syntax is politics, the economy
production and loss

perhaps grieving
is good for the system—thing versus
no thing

one versus the boundless flood

'the book
held together with strings' (Norris, K.

Zen, haiku, koan

the railway has now removed all its rails
between here and the border

take the train

xvii)

Year of the Rooster, a crow
in the cold dawn

                luck

after the bust, the boom
                        and soon
the living will outnumber
the dead

*cinq cent millions de Chinois
et moi et moi et moi*

the market ain't seen nothing like it
since the Cambrian explosion

chickens
coming down like snow

and the unemployed, the unemployed

and death in the interim
cheaper than aspirin

one of those endless commodities
provided by the free market for the pursuit
of happiness

then, of course
the millenium: honeycombed millions
in *domotique* cells

the earth mainly parkland offering
bizarre items, like weather

what was it like, together
waiting, did they kiss
the knees of the rails

xviii)

confess: their names are gone
with the recycled papers

now is sunlight, snow
blank as a new diskette

so end

tomorrow to fresh fields
and pastures new

but the old burden nags, of guilt
of rage

these things go on
like the weather: one begins
with ends

xix [Reprise]

is this necessary, the yearly
sacrifice of lambs

sparagmos

the tearing apart of bodies

as if a pride of lions left, replete
scraps for the jackal

is this the only ancient route to
communion, breaking the image, breaking the fast
the body of this death, discreetly
in board rooms

these small bodies in their winter clothes

in editorials

or is this road kill, silly deer
that wildered walk into the eye
of the machine

A THOUSAND

HOODED EYES

(Reprinted from *A Thousand Hooded Eyes:*
Poems by D. G. Jones, Coloured Wood Engravings
by Lucie Lambert. Les Editions Lucie Lambert
Vancouver/Shawinigan, 1990)

i)

The universe is a largely
dry subject, but water, o thalassa,
that is a matter

of imagination, its trickles, runnels, vast
littorals suspend
almost a page of elements

a soup, a salty sea
of discourse, it can generate
strings of sunlight, diatoms, flatworms

those wavering
soft lightbulbs (Medusa, Noctiluca) &
the glass catfish

ii)

which came first, the stomach
or the appetite to process
watery bits

o bricoler, o bricolage
let's cover the bag with scales, let's
hang it on a line

detecting tremors
let's make our own
waves, add fins

finesse, add bite
add sinister, voilà, the pike, the clown
the surgeon fish

iii)

a bad day for Beelzebub, his
minioned flies
                        out of
pond matter
the belly aspires
spawns legs, the spatulate
fingers, smiles

and slippery (I love
the frogs in your jacket) dines
and climbs

replacing bee's buzz
click and drone, with the piccolo & the heavenly
trombone

iv)

the Pentagon is the simple
beginning of the turtle, the amateur
of armoured plate

provide, provide
by pushing everything aside
for the retractable

fat legs, and beak—and double it
above, below
miz and mister five by five

add packaging, the eggs transporting
sea water, the beachhead
with a thousand hooded eyes

v)

the crowned
salamander of the French
kings hides

in pockets with keys (these rings
for sale
at Chenonceau

maintained
by a manufacturer of fine
chocolates) O

sweet lizard, lockets of queens
could not contain your royal
meanderings

vi)

certain African vipers are
a macramé angels
dream of, intricate

as the forest floor, where the pretty lumps
lie like angels
still, until the busy prey

passes, passing
into their design—few
are chosen, worse

few of those elect
become truly divine
in a lady's purse (or pumps)

vii)

the alligator's motherly
and builds a nest
of brush and stuff

she cracks small turtles with
unseemly zest

she stars in films where scientist
is evil genius—who
is breakfast in the end? (you guess)

she blends
kindness with her mortal ends: swallowing
she rests, that prey

may say their orisons

viii)

j'appelle au loin
—Paul Piché, *25/6/90*

where the twisted pines
split, in the inks of
Wei Yen, the pale bones

of tigers and dragons
—according to Tu Fu, there being
no other evidence

tonight
in Québec, the dragon is white
and blue, the

evidence ten thousand
flags in the wind, the supple
spine of song

ix)

lives in old books or
manuscripts, in
the orient

in the Chinatown
of Amsterdam, ka-bam!
outdoes

for a day
the prostitutes—a stately
clown—when other

fish, flesh, & fowl
are gone, he will swallow the stars
and lie down

SPOTS ON

THE CALENDAR

Like an Old Scholar

Like an old scholar, the garden
weaves us, each year, with birds
into a text more layered
                        winds
adding excerpts of cloud, traces
of new chemicals

headlines are absorbed like cat's bones
bent nails
              ads and perversions
all folded into some
Epicurean discourse

                 your flesh
figures a history of gardens

a stick myself, I shall harp on the infinite
ramifications of trees

the stars an occasional shudder

the moon, these chimneyed roofs, the slates
compost to this vegetating tome

Ode on a Piece of Cast Concrete
for Northrop Frye

The empty urn, the stalks
yellowing beside it, and apples
spilled on the terrace
                              anchor something
in the floating garden, after rain

The wooden bucket, on its side, once
held a story
                tipped, a summer
spills over

Let's say the denouement
unties the plot, boards rot, the air
humid

blurs the vista
                This is the quietus
of the ravished bride, blanks

and bits, odd props
which may precipitate desire, but are for now
enough

Add, if you like, yes
beauty is truth, and truth is this
articulate emptiness

Covering Letter

i)

It is not possible to cover everything: axlerods,
axeheads (Minoan civilization, Brébeuf's neck-
lace), action (the unities of, the rise and fall of
shares), acupuncture and acute accents, actuarial
statistics (and the General Services Tax on funerary
expenses), actually all we ask is that you cover
essentials—fig leaf, shroud ('I bought pearl neck-
lace and earrings, which she liked to wear in her
last years'), credit card—an abstract, the General
Acceptance Corporation. Adieu, earth's bliss; adieu,
Aphrodite; adieu, the remains. That covers it.

ii)

My mother dead, I write letters to a phantom limb.

iii)

Hosta. Gone yellow. The plantain lily hit by frost. And rocks, a
half circle. In this grey margin of my world, a necklace remains, a
coronal. Hosta and rock. No, it is the ring, the heavy ring, the ring
broken. It is an old testament.

iv)

Florida, *venereal soil*. Hardly. She lies under palms in that sandy
spit. Some friendly bones at her side. Here it rains *in her memory*.
Hardly! Covers it rather in folios of wet leaves. That book *Le
Tombeau de*—her phantom tomb.

v)

The frail wrist, looking to touch the friend, name
forgotten, yet known, dear Florida Cracker—wrist was right.
Remembering such a few touchings across a continent of life.
Remains here a bracelet ... about the absent bone.

vi)

Heavy soils and rock, remember thee. Like a strange language. In
the other country. You touched, uncovered, bones in the cold
parts, between river and rock face, rain turning to snow. Without
epitaph.

vii)

No I.D. Here, which is again elsewhere. This bracelet is broken, is
woman's, is earth's, is nameless. She has slipped all covering letters.

viii)

Coronal.

Preparing for Winter

the rocking chair on the porch
in a surf of leaves

so many things to be disposed

—whoever sat there anyway

the Maclennans, Hugh and 'Tota'
doddering, and exclaiming
how green it was
                    the poignant
moment in a farce (I think
they slept in their clothes

—and garden tools, and the hose

they were distracted from their ends
by a young lady's marriage

as we were, yes, and by things
to attend to

we attend—expect, wait for
Terror and *Erebus,* the tide—it sounds
oddly like the beginning
of *The Cantos*

and the Northwest Passage opening
blankly on the lawn

no matter, remains
are always disposed of, a matter
of turning the page

what an awkward beginning to end with
like spring

The Ship as Navigator

five boards from a pine
precede
and outlast me

I have lived
with my elbows on this table

and pots and pans
and papers

idiot life! sun and moon
wars, computers
mini-skirts, long skirts, knee-length
—holy jeans

and lilies, day and species
nights
with a last Scotch

my raft amid the galaxies, themselves
fleeing like refugees

winters of Saint Denys-Garneau
blizzards
from all sides, some
appleblossom

night turns
on this coordinate

a kitchen chair, some cracked
refurbished boards

Pumpkins

pumpkins survive like the devil

halloween, and the dead are lounging
all over town

like farmers in winter, flushed by the fire, easy
and idle

autumnal otium

the weightlessness of these straw-men
women, gap-toothed, slack
is a parody of the right stuff

not a whimper

they surround themselves
with abundance, indifferent, knowing nothing
like Buddhists

naturally, that inspires children, flames
the untold wickedness
of living

some pumpkins, of course, understand, their heads
full of candles

Bliss Carman, I Remember You Died the Year I Was Born, And

this was your weather
love and the flying leaves one
submission, riotous amid
the ruin of empire
and the pungent odour of decay a gold
meltdown—so
the lovers humping it, live for the crowd, the
shifty innumerable dead
the tall waif and his bouncing
matronly 'star,' their blithe
eurythmics, all
a tumbled operation of bodies
twigs in their hair, knees and marbly
civilized buttocks printed
with foliage, Pan, I suppose
beating the bushes, tossing
birds to the sky—how often, how many times
I ask can you play
death and the resurrection, put on
your boots (sneakers
tennis shoes) and stride through the broken
arbor to your bare room, an all new
November, you, now
part of the forest floor
                              I hear the wind
how it pours through the branches
and the news
from the broken cities—your reply, I presume
as I too
walk into the stripped, stupendous sky

Another View of the Bird

blue himself and half snow
the jay enjoys it, winter
the flight of capital, small clouds, cold sky
latitudes of childhood

yes, yes, he flashes about
like a policeman round pubescent hills
blanched roofs, a dazzled slit
of water
       he inspects
gaps, gone mirrors where the trees, stripped
act out their silences

is brief, as certain clouds
turn pink, then rufous at the edge
then grey

arrested, his prehensile toes
padding a branch, he eyes
berries
      the branch, the whole bush
bending beneath him
sways
      we laugh
seeing his beak open, hearing his cry
like a sprung latch

Towards the Chinese New Year

shapes rise from the hedge like bread rolls

and the roofs of the houses have been whimsically
warped, their deep eaves lined
with faint, undulant strata

winter, with a child's blue
awash in the sky

the wind, the lights and the shadows

let's say a man of sixty-five
is released into some kind of sketching class
some plastic dimension

birds, yes, scribble the intervals
without record
               unless
the tangled thickets, leafless, mime
their virtual messages

now I know why Ni Tsan travelled
among the white lakes
                         learning to breathe himself out
with the fading shoreline, a pure
virtuality, open
perhaps to a tree, a mountain, some small figure
fishing in the washed sky

An Inspiration of Ducks

at a certain age one rejoins
the company of animals

despite the cold, the dog says
let's go look at the ducks

five or six , on a spit of effluent, flick
water over their backs—orange
webbed feet—stiff-jointed, half-
extended wings—shake themselves
preen, like kids at a water hole, some
family on the Ganges

except the ice forms like shadows
from the piers of the bridge
—tongues of black glass to navigate
gently

        but there are others
they come up stream in squadrons
the river a moving
illustration of interference, V's
spawning V's, some
threshing the water with their bills
to feed
            only the flow
keeps the river from freezing

right, says the dog, more interested in smells
than feathers in water

but I think, nosing our way home
perhaps humans can live there
in hyperspace, where the temperatures
are well below freezing

Listening to Satoshi

A stone, he says, is a bag of sand
You can cut it like a loaf
with a diamond saw

Crazy man, he finds
barn lights, a winter's dawn
driving to the stone works

As well piss in a pail
          except the toilet affords, shit
idiot graffiti

Jackhammers, stone saws, sandblasters
metal on stone, chain lift and
flatbed, din, an

eight hour shift, say it, he does
time in pandaemonium
industrial rage

red-eyed with granite dust
—to make this silk shard, this hard
silent line

For Pien Wen-chin & Max Loehr

the specialists, painting flowers
or birds
          they were often exquisite
says the scholar
but a bit much when nature
is turned into an aviary

so much for today's garden
full of snow and light and
chickadees
          though
not a scroll so much as a score

notes flit up and down the scale in a brilliant silence

I suppose it's a bit like watching
one of those mechanical pianos
with the sound turned off

for a quarter of an hour maybe
in the clear cold

a ditty, perhaps, like
'Anything Ming can do I can do better'

or something by John Cage called
'Three-Tree Concerto for Wintering Birds'
to be played *sordino*

Blue Girl

there is no wind, no moon, only
this print about Modigliani
about a girl he had something
to do with, in blue—whatever cafés,
rooms in Paris, nights
in Canada with no moon, only
the blue girl, the normally absent
painter, the young woman who writes
in some room about some
piece of paper ... and the faint
sound now of some plane crossing
this blank space—possibly in
moonlight, in the jet-stream, the pilot
logging the hours, precise
location in air—it is winter
still, though mild, dark, silent now
and I do not know where to place
the blue girl or the writer
writing so intimately about the
blue girl she never, no more
than Modigliani ever, or I ever
knew

Last Things

this bird's skeleton, a few
feathers still attached to
each wing, might have exercised
St Ignatius in his meditations
(a form of home video on
the ultimate orgasm, worms
and the purge)
                    the thing
might interest someone at the Smithsonian
as an exercise in reconnaissance (Quick
a Mig or an F-16?) I mean
it could be a Phoebe

ashes tend to be ashes, though the urns
vary—some like cookie jars
some like shell cases, some like rare
glass lachrymaria

my own guts, skewered or incinerated
interest no one (not even me)

this bird starved and was picked clean
by the flies—neat, eh?

Fin de Siècle Springtime Ramble

The lake ice has become a shimmer of clouds, the dark, the light, the no-cloud—water's estates. A heavy slab of hill floats there. Here a crow flaps through the bric-a-brac, trees, wires, poles, a drift of roofs, a world adrift.

The world conceived as wreckage. The 20th century conceived as wreckage, the drifting remains of empires, economies, ideologies— bodies scattered on hillsides, washed over flood plains, stacked in the killing fields, hidden in boneyards, abandoned in parks or in parking lots, dumped in an alley. All part of the floating world, singed letters, sodden scripts, broken clichés—tablets, timbers, of temples and shrines, the law and the prophets—bibles, torahs, sutras, holy korans, handbooks of reason, catechisms of science— Newton's Principia, Kant's Critique—the colours leaching in the cartoon angels and devils, the lines softening in the crabbed anatomies, the forms of the papier-mâché heroes and villains and architects of the universe swelling and dissolving.

We have seen it, the fire, the flood, the ice. Now it seems like spring. To hear the sound of a truck on the road. To walk out into silence. To discover a world, the fading sound of an engine, of a crow amid wreckage, the lake ice subsiding, making a dull boom under the weight of the rain and the melt water. The crushed arks, cod bones and road kill—the smell of this detritus. And we are awash in a world of information, the lake ice becoming a shimmer of clouds, dark, light, no-cloud—water or air, beer can or plastic. The crow's caw shredded by bric-a-brac. Gibraltar dissolved, says Stevens, like spit in the wind.

We stand on the shore, or the edge of the drifting plates, as the funeral pyres burn to an ash and the ashes drift in telluric winds. We stand on the shore and the coffin ships move out on the tides and dissolve in the silence—the tides of information, short waves and long waves and lightwaves of a certain duration. And, for the moment it's spring, and we walk out amid wreckage—and some- one gives suck to a baby, someone discovers a poem in a bottle, someone discovers that chaos is order—the clouds in the ice and the water in air. And someone says these are the shimmering scales of the dragon. And someone says no, these are the elements we work with, these and the silence. Today, says another, you may walk in the clouds, you may walk on the water. These sounds in the silence, in the fin de siècle, in the spring, when the crow says, listen, here's the song of a truck.

The Bath

the bath, from Diana to Degas
the body that comes as an accessory
with every Jacuzzi

is never private

ask Susanna, ask
Agamemnon or Hitchcock's
lady in the shower

washing away the sins of the world
and towelling dry

—the pipe wrench in the dream
of mirrors and marble
sexual plumbing

here now, and the toilet upended
among bits of plaster, wood splinters, tile
the joints and couplings, hair
from the clogged drain, even
a tortoise shell brooch

oh, Susanna—yes, and the elders
stripped of desire
you are here like a trace

like a boot print left
in the dust of the moon, *le voyage*
à Cythère

The Darling Buds of May

This wind is possible because the ice
melted the breath of ferns—a boy and girl spill
their hot breath, naked in grass
on Mrs. Virgin's hill, because the ice
melted, breathing trees—their tongues
taste like things remembered in the sea
'lovers in their ordinary swoon,' like adders
twisting on their shed skins
and like and like, their souls
glistening in the nerve ends, 'it has been going on
for a long time,' the ice still melting
round the poles, this wind
shaking notes like blossoms from the chimes
hung in the apple tree— what should an elder do
with all this *spiritus*—some child
within the old reptilian brain still sees
the nubile body as a door
to watery gardens and with his mouth there
he would breathe like Ali Baba
'Open Sesame'—like Alice reading
'Eat me,' reading 'Drink me,' like and like
why can't an old man clear his mind
or clear his desk—or clear that mess
of still green leaves the wind has shaken
from the crippled elm—what does he do
with all this *spiritus*
but blacken paper—why can't
he let his mind go, be
an old body in the wind, the sound of ice
melting, air
divested of its trees and leaves, its touching chimes
similitudes of grass in grass
catastrophes—he doesn't hear, he's joined
the old men short of breath in bushes
round a bath, upon a hill, who gasp
it's like and like and like—the rake, if you please
the rake, I said
it's time to clear the yard

Quoting Lives

A leaf threaded by some insect
to a chair is like
a friend's life

or like a phrase

smale fowles maken melodye
that slepen al the nicht
with open yë
         attached
to the memory of a summer night, a dawn
beside a river
and a birth, where all one does
is wait

metonymies, the leaf
suspended in the imperceptible
currents of the air

and twirling, a seeming
dessicate activity
         and yes, some spider syntax
sutures the aporia between
the quick / the dead

as birds, this evening, merely
ruffle leaves

A Darkness With Eyes

the dog has broken the lilies and crawled
through juniper, cedars

she is wedged between the house and the garden
like a root between stones

a hurt—or more simply an animal
trying to die

The Sense of Paradox

thinking of snow when birds
beggar sound in the leaves and
it might rain

the cat buried in full stride, even as it was
when hit

'frozen motion'

the plants: daylilies, hosta, the pink
impatience, foaming from a bowl, so much
still life

so on certain days the snow falls without motion

so, windless, the world
becomes impossible to think

no rain, no snow
no comment, only
opposites collapsing—just hold your breath, it's all
feast and famine

Reading the Grass

what happened to romance
the summer idyll
         I mean
we're down to the last dog in
dog days and it's an exertion
just to flick one's ash in the shade, the sun
over the yardarm
        clink!

mushrooms, yes, they're back
on the lawn, the brown ones
that go moldy-white then black
and liquify

like a rotting accordion, a polka
in extremis

time to bury the summer with the cat
and another colleague

no more reading of poems
at funerals, lines that purport
unwonted sense: winter images that come up
poppies, also black

nothing stirs in the grass, but the text
is corrupt

To a Single Mother

this devotion to one life will
tear you apart—one must love
outrage
        failure
                keep betting
the world will be fine, will be fine
like a song

in your flowered leggings you look like the thirteen-year-old
    I remember drilling
youngsters to march up and down
the garden wall

You are not
sadder and wiser, though older
but younger again

in love

wide-eyed, the kid takes in dogs, gangs
whites, blacks, men with gold chains on their tanned
chests, women whose hands
are all rings, little girls with their mothers on a suspicious
merry-go-round, racketing boys making a foray
through the dusty park—thunder
and yachts in the background

innocent trouble
                all possible songs
reckless love or lonesome heart
or diamonds, darling, are all you've got

success perhaps the last seduction—any way
it is loss
the normal motor of desire, of hope, since the first
mother, love now premised
on a separation
                and that, not salvation, is
66   the good news

Another Snow Job

the hedge is full of moon flowers
lunar fauna, monsters the snow makes
you won't find these, I tell myself
in Disneyland
                    and I saw a bust
of Venus in the lamplight

compensation, you say, sublimation

civilization, says Freud—and hey!
I didn't cook this up, that
half white stabile is a real
apple tree—no papier mâché sets
in this yard
                    let's say
a kiss before dinner is better than seeing
a star on the beach
in Miami

so one tells oneself, and it's also
probably true

even when the pipes freeze for ten days

how to live on a pension requires
imagination

or simple perception
Paul Auster writes of a solitary character holed up
in some winter mesa, 'bit by bit
the world became enough'—a strange
statement, oddly, most of the time
not true

HOW TO PAINT IN

THE RECESSION

i)

note the happy vagueness
of rain and falling leaves

the neatness of cropped plants
yellowing, how things
go in and out of focus

the juncos, for example, foraging
in the half-raked grass

transient

to be pasted up with disasters
from the weekend papers
and a windfall of utopian writing
from job applicants

remember
some details of your will include
the off-colour splendour
of this yard

            your lawyer
may not buy it, but I put it to you
seriously, a life is a collage

ii)

what Chinese painter made it a principle
never to paint when sober

Colville, I presume, paints with milk

a hard way to get at the jaundiced
complexion of certain plants, the apoplexy
of Astilbe, or simply
the whole range of intoxication that sweeps
through this neck of the woods in the wake
of the wild geese
                    still
it takes at least a pair to make a world

Colville painting himself and his wife
naked in the light of the fridge

and Sung masters, maybe sober, painting
mountains and rivers with, sometimes, human specks
climbing or fishing

only too often the new art of installations
seems colourless
                    consider this
someone has jacked up an old car
and is taking it apart in the rain
and though some of the trees are bare
the wrecked garden, the whole
autumnal installation clanks and
flickers with humours
green bile, yellow bile, dried blood, a hectic
body cast for video with smoke
and strange transparencies

some of course prefer black and white
and we'll get to that (ink stone, tombstone
snow

for the moment I'll opt for scotch and a brush with a keyboard

iii)

Vogue is useful and even better
is *Architectural Digest*, if you've got any
rich friends and can afford
glue and scissors

bits of everything: drabs
like fallen leaves of the basswood
jewelled effects of rain-wet
cankered willow leaves, ebony
on a gold laque

then rusts, or the wispy thrums
of blonde grass

a spectrum of deliquescent shades
or something brilliant, a lost
blue jay's feather

you're working on a small scale
but it's the best money can buy—the scattered
radiance of eternity—paid for
by fashion

and so, so, there's something grey
in the mirror, that too
you can find
                    update Lautrec
or *The Portrait of Dorian Gray*, or Rembrandt's
gold in the gloom, *The
Alchemist's Dream*, or mock up some splendid
auto-da-fé

or jubilate, do
Mandelbrot variations in *Vogue*
forest to fig-leaf to sequin
in fall colours, we'll call it
fractal co-ordinates

iv)

baseball has closed down
the daily catastrophes, it's pouring
and the dog loves it

the arthritic are happy that a young man's
as crazy as the dog and likes
walking in the rain

one delays dying
like those African cattle herders who delayed
their spring migration to catch
the end of *Dallas*

in pluviam felicitas: the fish
enjoyed the Flood

are there nymphs of Fall: like those girls Carman met, losing their
leaves, one step ahead
of the sun's shadow, bathers
in the cold rain, fish-faced, a whole troupe
called The Mocking Ophelias

do they mess with dogs, outfielders
or the strolling orphic youths
adrift in the suburbs

older, older, can one paint an autumnal
'Garden of Delights,' maybe rename it 'Woodstock Revisited'

or, *en plein air*, this weather, simply use cutouts
of bodies, of bushes, with a sign
WET PAINT!

v)

for something to happen, something's
got to stop happening

there's a lot happening, says the foreign
correspondent, the war
stretching into another winter

Kaffe Fasset, he sure gets around
stitch by stitch—I mean, for me
this is news

the painter who took to knitting

so I discover M on the sofa
surrounded by balls

the weeds die, the phlox and the cosmos
that brain rack, Angelica
making things happen, and there is a certain
harmony of dyes

kaffee klatsch, with Fasset the bassett
hanks and testes of yarn, or
as they say in Québec, *les p'lotes*

I'm not selling anybody's product, but the guy
clicks off a woolly
diapason—and he only asks of the sheep
they get sheared—the haircut
as a pastoral symbol
                          other happenings
cost you your life

vi)

a windfall inheritance, this gold
of the maples, or in these times as good as
a pay cheque
                and spent
before the wind comes

an autumnal economy, and wearing

first a bonanza, then veins
of capital (deep pockets, old money) striating
the depressed hills, then
not much

the consolation of November is
shared poverty
                a landscape
neglected by ad men

meanwhile we make what we can
of ashes, the bone-coloured branches
bark like old pennies, water
, like a service of pewter, a wealth
of greys and infinite dinginess

the high rollers, the big-time
spenders are gone
                and the banks
whether royal or mere *caisses populaires*
can reassure us: we lose our
customers honestly
one at a time

vii)

politicians falling from office, leaves
from their branches, make
I suppose, rich compost

and the weatherman tergiversates
maybe rain, maybe snow
but windy for sure, yes, and for sure
cold

despite electoral change

there is a rhetoric as immortal
as plastic flowers

the actual garden looks like a graveyard
flowering with markers

and the calendar says honestly
The Day of the Dead (lively
with pumpkins) and

Remembrance Day, with its rusted tanks
artillery—its plates, its plaques, its walls
of names

the constant between parties

here, I picture my aunt
on a bridge in November, amid bayonets, placing
a wreath on the snow

viii)

is it better if deer
nibble the neighbour's old
apple tree or will
the house insurance go up

do jets resonate more clearly
in colder air, like Orion
the hunter (his horn, though, mute
as *le cor de Roland*

death and triumph mix
like the media, a simple leaf
curled at the edges becomes
an embroidery

some are made beautiful at last
in their bones

such obscure
clarifications, the hard head
reduced to a hero, leaves
to their veins, flights
to their vapour trails

traces
        dying
is a form of refinement, the Fall
high pastoral

ix)

can you paint the wind, the loss
of jobs, the vacancies
mocking November

like a dog nosing grass, layered leaves
an impasto of deadfall, the light
leaden on the far lake

the bitch seems happy enough
in this desolation (horses leave cold
mud as a mark

what she smells
are traces, animals no longer there

and the night wind
the temperature rising accords
oddly

with the climate of investment

great trees fallen over the path
the bank eroded

is that memory, her brow
furrowing over the eyes

hound dog, what does she know
couched on a sofa
can she smell it, the rich passage
of devastation, of rain, rot
the wasted

it's a dog's life, as we say
as post-industrial progress
winnows the world

x)

greetings, I've just read
they've invented
blue roses
            hope you're enjoying
your latest divorce

I mean now there's a future for the
half-unemployed, the part-time unhappy
the tearful successes who leave footprints
in the wet snow at the end
of november

perhaps they will thrive in the chequered shade
of trans-nationals
                        like the beggars
under the walls of the Vatican

and wolves will be shepherds

O genetic engineers, shall we dally with the shades
in fields of asphodel—are we there
already

—no, paint that out, no posies
no roses today

make your eye lonely
                        here
under the dead skirts of the spruce tree
on the glazed stones, in patches already
blanketed over, the moss, the lichen

ikebana with snow

xi)

wintering over: the caribou
pawing up green pastures, Laplanders milking
the reindeer

something to hang on the wall
as you tick off the days

                              a recession
may hit the equator, *la favela* in Rio
St Henri in Montreal

like it's an urban distemper often
with sunny days
sex and skinheads, booze and grafitti
these don't go away

rot comes in all kinds of colours

and there's crime, and the smart money
heading for Denver, the Caimans
planes for Bangkok, a deal
on abandoned artillery, there's always someone
owns a TV

someone there to explain
the structural imbalance, fingering
bad angels

during the Japanese occupation, I'm told
Ch'i Pai-shih painted shrimp

here we have sidewalks littered with acorns
a sour mash for the whisky
of wintering squirrels

xii)

morne, an appropriate
strong colour
as if the French
plundered the Goths for iron
not gold
or gold leaf

the colour of the times

not the feeling of a broker but the look
of the market

as with hunters, among dead reeds
one watches the bird
fall

the margin

c'est infime, itself
almost nothing

but an intoxification because the difference
is almost irrelevant or
loss as precious as gain

　　　　　　　　　　a joke

like nothing is wisdom
but to fly, to dance, to colour
—one loves the distraction, the least
holiday

morne

the impossible *hutzpah*, earth
laying bets with the sun

WHAT IS
INTERESTING

i)

the wise man can say turn up the heat
when the wind blows or put a blanket
on the fire, a blizzard says think twice
again and again and again

the epigram hits the nail on the head, the
koan hits the student on the head, the
enigma says where is the nail

the blizzard is brainstorming, man is a snow
says Birney, that cracks
the tree's resinous arches—is he, then, also
water made wafers
or cornflakes, or leaves from a kind of whitethorn
blossoming ghostly, a mirror of spring
as fertile as language covering
and reworking earth

the waves, says Pierre, after passing the graveyard
in squalls—what did he say (we'd moved
to ashes as a conversation piece), the waves
suggest heroic acts (we are driving
through a pastoral landscape, still
the virtue of ABS brakes is that they compensate
for unequal resistance, like the *tao*
or the free market, I mean
this is a lake in a blizzard in december
in canada, metaphor is in the shape and lick of the waves
and their *pompe et funèbre* hue, whew! the rest
is metonymy, hanging in there
in difference) the picturesque
becomes the sublime, you could die in this
preparation for a white Christmas, this
greeting card

what is interesting is skidding from snow
to ashes to blossoms, greetings
of dark jubilation, the waves, the waves now the clapping
of an excellent tragedy

ii)

it was Christmas and the pub was closed
and the gift shops, and the people strolled
round the lake wondering what to do
or stood on the bridge and looked at the ducks
in the steaming river
                              quack

and here was death
walking the dog

and the sun would soon go under the hill
under a cloud

                    and the gulls were returning
to roost on the waves, folded, adrift
in their undulent mirrors

and some girl walking her new man recognized me
saying, Hi and
Merry Christmas
                    and I recognized
the philosopher coming off a sort of pier
where I presume he'd been trying to stare down
the unphilosophical waves and said
Merry Christmas in such a confident voice
I'm sure he was quite surprised

the word epiphany has a meaning
in opposition to cover-up or
obfuscation, but here
in the snow, where death walks the dog
in broad daylight and lovers
say Hi
        everybody loves
a fat bitch wagging her tail

                    I mean now
should I stare at those hyaline waves and confess
I see through a glass darkly

iii)

mysterium tremendum
there it is in its resonating Latin syllabubbles
like clouds, like clouds
of silent thunder

like mommy in the bath or
daddy in the shower

especially if he can sing *O sole mio*

and the snow comes like a new
flourescent lighting
to dispel and to deepen, to awe
and to wow us, oh
it's like going snowblind at the sight
of a loved person
naked
      don't we go cosmic
discovering then we are one
with the expanding universe, the beloved
betraying a red shift, discovering
desire, discovering
anxiety, one
and a part

the lake, its waves and its wavelets, little sprays and
    little splashes, little drops, is a flare
one looks from the window and where there was water
    there is nothing but light, blinding

and remember the conjugal pair in Joyce's *The Dead*
    the flakes falling around them, falling on Dublin
    falling on Galway and graveyards and breakwaters
    and the waves of the sea, apart and together in a
    kind of queen size, white, and dissolving bed

so, so, such snow-white choirs shall sing thee to thy rest

O sole mio amid the whirls and drifts
of syllabubbles, these foaming
sentences of light

iv)

the lake freezes and the days grow longer

the jet stream moving south, we enjoy
an arctic air mass, the next best thing
to cryogenic preservation

a thin snow, a milky sun, and the trees
shifty with chickadees, chickadees
and a nuthatch

the souls of the houses spill out of chimneys
like turbulent children, the world
their blank page
                        let's doodle
let's babble, this silence like sunday
this lake like a stilled drum

boom

and the nights join in, ice mimes the sky
with fissuring thunder, trees crack
nails pop, we have sniper fire in our own
resinous arches

destiny is about us, the satellite air
filled with news of floods and improbable births
and the number of killed and wounded
in a city
frozen in falling
                        like the invisible
text of the birds, arabesques, unfoldings
in the milky light of the sun and the milky
light of the moon, grace notes themselves
in the interstices
of the branching night

and late, late, if one scrunches one's eyes
the Christmas tree lights figure forth the galaxy in human shape
cold spaces and raging fires suddenly quiet
with colour and the rustling of birds

v)

beauty is not practical, snow
on the lilac, hedgerows in white
and green, make work
at midnight (one is shovelling out
the car) breathless

and spontaneous affection is
equally dangerous or
merely ridiculous, your wife says
—it was New Year's Eve, the lady
a child once in Poland—you looked
like romeo
haranguing juliet, you
on your retiring knees
                              these antics
are part of the cosmos

like a guest, who arrives at the party
saying I just pulled a woman
out of a burning car, and today
S arrives saying I just
pulled a man out of a car, I think
he had a cracked pelvis

in the midst of the sublime, someone
has a bad cough—and don't forget
to walk the dog

vi)

hours of still falling snow
then the tall pines in a bit of wind
collapse, like a space station slowly
coming apart

this is the beauty of smoke
broken by smoke in a wrecked
civilization
                this is the beauty of a *fête*
champêtre in the Townships
at 20 below

the beauty of *is* in transition, brief
as some bits in a video

                        small birds
making minor adjustments

elsewhere ships go down, elsewhere
houses float their rooves into flames
elsewhere good goods make a floating bazaar
the sublime become news

the phantasmagoria dissolves
like a forest after fire
                        leaving snow
on a dead channel

                        whatever's out there
might be the holy ghost

vii)

another variation, perhaps
on the thirty-some names for snow

the muse of the true north
strong and free

or shall we speak of a white-out
as orgasm, of the jouissance
of first flakes on exposed skin, of making
angels in snow
purdy depressions, the archaeology
of heavenly bodies

the wind comes up, freezing the gas line
a little touch
of something in the night

what is interesting should be profound
like an iceberg, a relic
of millenial snows, the great
glacial word
            layers of sweet nothings
little kisses of crystal, like celestial
millefeuilles
          ah, the French
with all their concern for dulia
hyperdulia and latria, they have neglected
la neige, they have elucidated
la cuisine, they have laboured to reveal
the thousand and one names
of wine
        its body, its nose, its communion
with rocks and trees and the fruit
of the sun and the rain
             JHVH
should scour and gride
              voilà
the car starts with a roar, and N takes off in a cloud
of carbon monoxide

viii)

winter or WNTR, with a fire
one can almost remember the world
of one's own body, alone
in its fur

        bear, brrr, berlin

and the snow speaks like a Buddhist
kindly

ms connelly notes our capacity
to make something of nothing, explanations
of mysteries, truth of the air

so death is a musical rest
in the dream of the bear god, time out
to play
        flowers become snowflakes
wind but a mouthful
of disaggregate vocables, whooay
strewing virtual garlands on the torso
of yesterday's discourse, old scores
liberated in improvisation

as the Thai monk said to the girl
it's like raising chickens
take the eggs and leave the shit

profundities of chicken feathers, snow
and its prophecies
          what's interesting
is what you can make of it, here
in this outpost of empire, margin
of some stellar inferno—to die
like a true Canadian, saying here's your chance
at negentropy, pucker your lips, compose
a candid rhetoric, saying
cool, man, cool, this is virginal
paradise—renaming the beasts

ix)

the sun goes down and the west
turns fuchsia

      winter flowers

the lake is nothing, for miles

what is the colour of a wedding gown
in the dark, of a shroud

these are things we know little about
in the centres of empire

winter hits us with a hike
in car insurance, the rush to get out new
spring fashions, escape

to death in Miami

here things are plain, for a time
the ten million words and the three thousand tongues
are reduced to a sigh
and an O

night and a no-colour body, snow
waiting for snow

x)

there's been a paradigm failure

the signs drifting down, piling up
emptied of difference
erase the surround

                    infant
one begins with the sound
of a footprint, one's weight on the snow
the intimate body

something brushy, eyes
at the end of one's arm
                              something moving
a bird, vision
perhaps the size of the yard

a bit of a chimney says colour

vague blocks, a wedge like a piece of meringue
make a house

a commotion of fur and of paws and of snuffling

here we have dog

how shall we bear these emerging relations

woof! we shall shake up the world

xi)

the world will shake us, as the wind
shakes out trees, a horizon

small fisherman crouched on the ice

as words shake out stories, old books
shake out mountains
pagodas and dragons, a lost girl
a hero
          someone says god
and you look into clouds and prepare
to be shaken

                and the snowplow
goes by and it shakes the whole house

watch out for the chicken shit

shake yourself off like the dog coming in from the cold

not much in *Careers and Professional*
but with satellite service
we'll have dozens of channels

so many directions, so many plots
for the unemployed

and the Olympics comes on full of fjords
and incentives to travel

at night, your bare feet on the floor
say it's cold
              that is good

and the wise man shuffles off
in your dream, saying
which way do you go through a door

xii)

never trust wise men with riddles

the stars that fall out of a film

TV evangelists

you're better off back where you started
going hooo in a blizzard

the epics of war, the romance
of technology, lyrical skin cream and promos
for cyberspace sex
mu'adhadhin or the boys selling crack

the ghost written futures

thirty-five million unemployed in the West
will meditate, still
in the pursuit of excellence, souls
quiet as hedgehogs white
in the lamplight

xiii)

one can say that fresh snow
always brightens things up
like a war

or an invasion of jargon (a statement to members
of a limited partnership speaks
of something expensed

watch out for what's buried

a man and his snowmobile just capsized
caught a beam that was framing
an old garden plot

globalization blanks out
the local particulars
                    a thaw
may produce holes in the argument

the path is uneven

pronto, vite, quick, snell
        ad hin und her and all together, ein
funf, zwei, sieben

zo, voilà, and oops! we learn
to stagger—falang, peasant—miracoloso

gracefully

LIKE FISHING

IN WINTER

i)

after the deep freeze, wind chill
pushing it to minus sixty
we get snow
                after three hours shovelling
one says it's warm

there was an earthquake in Los Angeles
but here it is still
                an apple tree
becomes a Sung classic, the intricate
anatomy of Yin
                the hedge
a range of mountains

as art, we have nothing to say

except the dog comes in, grinning
a bone in his jaws like a mouthful
of diamonds

ii)

today is brilliant, the photographer
plows up the bank to discover
the wind has knocked the hell out of
a Chinese masterpiece
                    oh
a trunk, a truncated arc, webbed groin
remain, but the arabesques
the intricate sprays, the floating
nodules, synapses
are gone
          it has the fascination
of a collapsed freeway

one gets on with one's business

towards sundown one glimpses
the lake through wreckage, surprised
at the delicate pinks and greys

iii)

driving out of the village I notice
the tombstones
up to their ears in drifts and all
wearing conical hats

what a parade

recursive symmetry—or a Baconian
essay
'Of Slabs and of Snowflakes'

weathering memory

meanwhile let's get to the bank
deal with the debts and domestic
necessities, these cars
spinning their wheels

—yet the drill in the graveyard
helps ... the old squares saying, hey
we're the Rockettes

iv)

death has a bad memory

keeps piling up the statistics and they don't
register, like Sisyphus
he props up another stone

as bad as the snow

the dog says piss on it, and does
wag, shake

in, out, back and forth between worlds, she's
content with a bone

and tiresome, barking at nothing

as we are, complaining
of new snow right after a thaw
new elegies—barking at our absent
shadows
            if
there's a fisherman on the lake
he's gone

I mean, it's like bad news is the only news
the sub-text a shroud

but again, the program aborts
it clears
and now we have two dogs
wrangling and bounding and irrepressibly
plowing up that perfect lawn

like two drunks at a wake, a mazurka
invading the requiem

I mean just when you think there's an end
nothing or OM, there's a glitch

v)

trees and snow in the clarity
of outer space, as cold
but with the added blue

Matisse arranging cut-outs for
la Gare du Nord

or an ad for *La Métropolitaine*
(insert photo and copy
                              Myriam Bédard
époustouflée en Norvège, avec
son petit fusil et ses skis mal accordés
à mi-chemin de la course
du biathlon

moving art or active
meditation

once, in such a decor, I recall
the dog getting snow in its paws and stopping
again and again, to lick them (the flaw
that authenticates memory

a different dog

be brief—we'll soon be into the flip side
of winter
              is this the splendour of Ionian
white and gold

uh-uh, this is explicable

let's just call it a retirement gift: a snow garden
sunlit, with its small birds

enjoy it, like a child

D.G. Jones is a poet, translator and critic. His books of poetry include *Balthazar and Other Poems* (Coach House Press, 1988). He won the Governor General's award for poetry in 1978 for *Under the Thunder the Flowers Light Up the Earth*, and for translation in 1993 for *Categorics 1,2,3* (both published by Coach House Press). He teaches at l'Université de Sherbrooke, and lives in North Hatley, Quebec.

Editor for the Press: Christopher Dewdney
Cover Illustration: bill bissett, detail from
figurs in a dreem (1989), oil on canvas

Coach House Press
50 Prince Arthur Avenue, Suite 107
Toronto, Canada M5R 1B5